The National Poetry Series was established in 1978 to ensure the publication of five collections of poetry annually through five participating publishers. The Series has been funded over the years by Amazon Literary Partnership, the Gettinger Family Foundation, Bruce Gibney, HarperCollins Publishers, The Stephen and Tabitha King Foundation, Lannan Foundation, Newman's Own Foundation, Anna and Olafur Olafsson, Penguin Random House, the Poetry Foundation, Hawthornden Foundation, Elise and Steven Trulaske, and the National Poetry Series Board of Directors.

THE NATIONAL POETRY SERIES WINNERS OF 2024 OPEN COMPETITION

Games for Children by Keith Wilson
Chosen by Rosalie Moffett for Milkweed Editions

82nd Division by D.M. Aderibigbe
Chosen by Colin Channer for Akashic Books

Blue Loop by AJ White
Chosen by Chelsea Dingman for University of Georgia Press

Our Hands Hold Violence by Kieron Walquist
Chosen by Brenda Hillman for Beacon Press

Shade is a Place by MaKshya Tolbert
Chosen by Maggie Millner for Penguin

BLUE LOOP

BLUE LOOP

AJ WHITE

The University of Georgia Press   *Athens*

Published by the University of Georgia Press
Athens, Georgia 30602
www.ugapress.org
© 2025 by AJ White
All rights reserved
Designed by Mary McKeon
Set in Bembo Book MT Pro by Mary McKeon

Most University of Georgia Press titles are
available from popular e-book vendors.

Printed digitally

EU Authorized Representative
Easy Access System Europe—Mustamäe tee 50, 10621 Tallinn, Estonia, gpsr.
requests@easproject.com

Library of Congress Control Number: 2025936887
ISBN: 9780820374314 (paperback)
ISBN: 9780820374321 (epub)
ISBN: 9780820374338 (PDF)

Here is the life that chose you / And the one you chose.

Robert Hass, "Art and Life"

Abandon even the desire to be free from desire.

Tilopa, *Song of Mahamudra*

Contents

BLUE LOOP

A *blue loop* is a stage in the life of a star when the star evolves from cool to hot before cooling again. Stars executing blue loops cross a graphical region called the *instability strip* because the outer layers of stars in this category are unstable & pulsate.

Blue stars are the hottest stars of all.

Time Anxiety

You loom suspended: sovereign
nimbi, sky-wide thresholds,

depthless, finer than cirrus,
vacant yet whelming

as the father-instinct.

✦

The past you cannot
see clearly, & the future

you cannot see through.

Dewdrops sublimating
like the names of the dead.

It will never exist,

the future you envision.
Only the dread

you will not learn in time.

PART I.

Semiprecious

Something will happen today, in white porch columned
       America, downtown, across the smooth & constant
river that runs, it seems, like I used to, for the sake of running,
       for the sake of being fast, feeling the world
as it is left behind, the absolute power of a stride,
       what my foot could do to a rubberized track,
put it in its place, leave it where I found it but lessened,
       & I am gone.

                 Something will happen later today,
& do you have this anxiety that I do, this semifrantic
       state of avoiding, at some great, unknowable cost,
ever being frantic, being out of control—have you ever lived
       one heartbeat to the next? I promise I'm not
trying to be dramatic. I assume you have, & do, & are.

Something will happen at 1:30 today: yesterday I said
       I am a free man, I should walk along the river, so I did.
There were omens: a raven's feather with its blue sheen,
       a Styrofoam bowl of macaroni & cheese
left on a stone wall, a newborn's white shoe. In the mall,
       where I went to be somewhere, legions of gold rings
bearing semiprecious stones in their neat rows & ranks,
       each so like a soul.

                 It helps to know the something
that will happen will not be the worst thing that has
       ever happened to a human being. Which is so selfish
it is perhaps more intolerable than what will happen.
       I keep waiting for the part of the story where I face
great hardship & emerge more benevolent & humble.
       I keep waiting for the part of the contest when I win.

Bewilderment

Nightfall, nowhere, late July—thunderheads come rummaging
          across the low folds of the hills, tufting
into the cup of the dell.
                    Freshly sparged, the open hands of the leaves
          say *YES, AND?* The sidewalk sighs.

The leaning beach umbrella in the neighbors' yard,
          sheltering the picnic table, flaps *YUP, YUP.*
                    Cardinals chase
each other into the cloister of nooks. The hinge-throated bird,
          a precognizant, is already long gone. The trees restless, ripe.

An American flag is wedged into a bush near the picnic spot.

From the attic of the cranium, a salt rinse, arrhythmic, spasming
          the oculus. Time blooms into a cavity,
                    a void aperture burgeoning
in the mind. I squeeze the lemon into tea, rinse a spoon.

Heedless, inevitable, coaxing the icepick back out,
                    the untethering shine hits
& I'm a needle shimmied into cork,
              clumsy atop a soap cloud—
          dizzy, spinning, homing in, bending round—

                 & I no longer recall if what I see—
stemware in the sink, power lines trancing up & down,

              the blood purse of my right hand—
is truly there or just need-projection,
              & I no longer know
if I have been living too carefully or not carefully enough.

Juniper

I wake up thinking about glass flowers
        on a wet afternoon in Cambridge,

half-lit mistruths
        lozenge-soft in their showcases:

glossy, fine-veined cherry blossoms,
        every stamen lash-thin,

impossible, each chamomile petal
        forever a glassblower's breath away

from wilting. I wake up sober six days
        facing a long weekend,

& out of doubt's cabinet rich
        with glass botanicals

I twist one single juniper berry
        from its needled stem

&, pausing for a moment, gulp it whole.
        Petal, nectar, seed—easy,

one after the next, I glug down.
        By noon I'm weightless,

halogen, Lite-Brite—toothy
        shards unsheathing

the mind-wiring, nerve fluid pooled
        like splayed glow stick.

Full Disclosure

Within the course of a few months, my calm, tall uncle
walked out into the pines, knelt down, & shot himself

in the chest—my titi drowned alone in her living room
in Little Havana, hundreds of cloth & ceramic cherubs

holding vigil from high cedar shelves around & above—
meanwhile in north Georgia my grandmother's mind at last

de-materialized across a barren, snow-kept causeway
onto a mineral sea, her eyes closed tight against the cold

passage, crying out in recognition,
from that place, of her own mother & father.

All recollection entails collection: autumn sun thins
like an old wound. Same year Benji swallowed his service

pistol. Same year dignity limped, finally, broken, wide
of my grasp. Holed up in motel rooms up & down

Appalachia, I drank as if I could preempt all my loves leaving
by ablation, sanding down the blade, dividing me by zero

& again. I survived, but left this outline there of my intent.
Some days the singe in my mouth of saltpeter & hickory coal

suggests I tread already as one of my own gone. Such proximity
is not unkind. Say that time & absence press by magnitude,

not, as we're told, by direction. There is no yet & past:
only gravities signaling I will see some of you soon.

A shocked dawn sears beneath the presidio
of my ribs. Say it will occur here.

The Suscitation of God

Someone has gathered together the sky—it is being folded
like a fitted sheet, imperfectly, into the bureau of the west.

Someone has dropped pigment into the horizon,
the way a pip of blood might leach into a porridge

or some waxy needles can be coaxed into a tea.
The emptiest vessel speaks the loudest,

& the earth is full of open mouths, but the sky—
& the way the trees bend,

the way the river gossips about you—
these things are permissions for a discourse.

& yet one remains perplexed—no one to sit you down
& say *that's enough for now, well done, rest.*

It's just me here, sobering up slowly, day by day,
wringing the damp from my underclothes.

Thinking you have arrived is ensnarement.
Thinking you have arrived, you may never leave out from home.

Luminous

Today I purchased a peach.
Actually two—one ripe, one less ripe—
each insistent as a boy's fist.

Sitting alongside each other
on the windowsill
they look bruised,
but they're just being peaches.

I spin one peach this way,
thumb thoughtlessly
its dark place, spin it back—
then I watch the sun's arms
pump its nectar into flame.

I have learned,
when you are bruised,
when you are desperate
to be permeated by light,

you open your pores to the careless,
who, in their cleansing,
shine into annihilation

even what you thought indelible,
what you believed
could not be erased.

We Were Never Really Going to Get Away

we had been apart a few months
the last time I saw you I let you
know I had been sober 8 weeks
for the first time in 8 years you
said fantastic we had coffee you
said you look good where did
you get that shirt you said do
you want to get a drink you
said you know we were never
really going to get away

I am still not sure if I have made
good my escape as we alcoholics
know each escape is a return a
reversion a plea to renegotiate
this hostage-taking knowledge
chiefly knowledge that we were
never really going to get █████

I will make a place for me yet
in the desert or by the sea
in the unattested silent
reverent place the place
to which we were
never really going
██ ██ ██

No More Stories, No More Meaning

a young rabbit in my childhood backyard I named Sorbet

lonely hours on the highway in west Texas passing no other car,
   only a headgate or two, & that sunset—a red tide, an ocean,

the soul's longing to go west, west, west, & never come back—

   when I came home from college & went to the coffee shop
or Kroger I always ran into parents from my high school—

   they always said the same things—are you pre-med?

are you going to law school? we can't wait to see what you do—
   here's what I do—drive drunk at 4am from one state

to another running away from yet another someone, yet

   another self, yet another commitment to get any help—
drunk in hotel rooms crying watching Miyazaki movies,

   crying watching *Room*, crying knowing I can't stop—

if they knew I am thirty years old lying in sweat & vomit
   in a motel in this hometown, stumbling down the street

to get another pint that disappears, stumbling across the trestle

   staring into the deep intravenous deoxygenated Oostanaula—
after I forget this, after my sister forgets this, after my mother

   & father forget this—will this still have happened to me?

Sobering

Here's how it happened:
first, I got arrested a second time.
The woman in the drunk tank with me, a grandmother,
had just run over & killed someone.
I'm sure I'm leaving something out.

First, I tried to drive through a telephone pole.
First, I tried to fall down some stairs.
First, the future grommeted my brain with blanks.

First, I called a lover ugly. First, I called a lover dumb.
First, a lover left me to die alone.

First, my grandmother's Parkinson's killed her.
First, my aunt's dementia killed her.
First, my delirium tremens tried to kill me
in a stranger's house. In a motel. In the ER.
In detox. In my car on the side of the road.
First, my uncle's gun killed him.
I'm sure I'm leaving something out.

First, I tried lots of NyQuil. First, I tried lots of Benadryl.
First, we got drunk in John's backyard
& everyone laughed at my jokes.

First, my parents never drank.
First, Aline Ray fled Chicago with her mother & seven sisters.
First, María Dolores Díaz Olmo sailed from Santurce to Miami,
seven years old, sent by her mother, who stayed behind.
I'm sure I'm leaving something out.

Later, I went to rehab. Later, I couldn't find god.
Later, I chose trees, clouds, & geese.
Later, I moved on from those I love who will not speak to me.
Later, I tried to move on.

Later, I learned to distract. Later, I learned to delay.
Later, I decided my excuses are not excuses
but avenues beyond wanting, toward knowing.

Later, knowing & I became acquainted.
Later, knowing told me you can want & not have
& that this is known as *life*.

Later, I took another path.
Later, I came back.

PART II.

Hostilities

I recall
staggering staring

through the Buddha
chanting wanting

field
of vision here to

rain white
I was getting sober

for the first time
practicing

acceptance chanting
look a mirror in

a niche
watch as I turn

back
into scarlet cups of

plunder comes
to some

of us
others only

bandits
here is my

museum where
I show you how

I ransacked all
I've gleaned

missiles stitches
spearpoints holes

revolting
too dizzy to

down further
starlight

Frog & Scorpion

we were at a party in Nashville I had
been trying to drink less so of course
I drank more ruined everyone's night
then I stayed up for hours whispering
in your ear *I hate you I hate you* until
you turned to me crying you had been
awake the whole time you asked why
I hated you & I did not yet know
it was because I hated myself because
at that time we were nearly one person
I had been out of work for months
drinking & drinking & anxious
for the first time & did not yet know
what was wrong with me which is still
here with me though you are not
of course because of all I would go on
to do to you & to others & then
only when there was no one else left
what I did to myself

The Act of Witnessing the Self-Containing Oath

We are in a kind of YMCA & kind of in prison, which is to say we are definitely in the YMCA's beige-white cinderblock, linoleum & parquet sweat/bleach glossy/dim interior, but, stepping outside, we are also definitely in a prison yard that is both a Jehovah's Witness compound & a zoo in Columbia, South Carolina, bountiful with magnolia & zooted capybara & fescue. The warden is a preternatural woman/being both fast & yet able to be seen from a distance stalking us across the verdant jeweled lawn & our task is to figure out which of these pavilion- or portico-like structures holds the gym facilities where we will be safe to shoot basketball.

Are dreams so hidden/hermetic/veiled? I am afraid of prison—have been held in a cinderblock jail; my grandfather spent most of my childhood in a prison. The warden is an ’Ερινύς [strife-raiser], one of three, who punishes offenders, those most deserving to be punished, who have committed [c]overt sins against the body/polis. I have spent time in both a zoo & a Jehovah's Witness compound in Columbia, South Carolina. What is the subconscious, anyway?

[our bodies spill/slink/squeeze in/amidst a groaning canal of bodies; a seeking lightning sizzles/flicks/surveils the surface; we run, not leg-like, cilia-like, stride/float/fleeing a red heat in the cold blue stream; cells in a body of cells under influence of a hunter/marauder/cell]

[dark liquid heat trills down her back peels off her side she is floodgate blood-tide her steps are wet hooved cloven her stag antlers dewy velvet brown dried blood her eyes gleam fire ash coal iridium she flows silver-wet into crevices of us we detonate from inside out vapor trapped in carapaces translucent slick airtight shells]

Today I sensed I was being mis-overheard, left *out in the open*. Oh, how powerless—I wake/come-to screaming/whimpering into the pillow *help help help!!!* wake at 4am to an automated email from the court & go back to sleep & dream this time I lose something very small, unholdable & easy to lose.

Silk

prison in the air

lake of salt on the sea floor

cryovolcano—magma encapsulated in ice

cumulus bioharvesting in the bloodstream

time dilation around the eyeball of a sun

a black hole is neither black nor a hole

it is the mouth of a river of energy

cloud an improvisation of bits

lustrous to observe

silk is harvested from moths without mouths

these are my spinnerets

words are harvested from me

I have no mouth

my larval form ate cruelty neglect

spun a prison in the air

to suffocate within

Only the Earth

I needed

fewer moving parts

an hourglass

has thousands

a sundial has only

the earth
—Kaveh Akbar, "Against Memory"

I needed a steady hand to wedge my head between that yesterheaven & the earth

fewer than sixty gins maybe fifty vodkas get me to commit my grotesque self has only

moving tumbling grimy portholes of perception panic vomit kaleidoscope a sundial

parts shade from brilliance halves prisms to banality takes sky's confessions has thousands

an hourglass whispers crystalline tidbits drips silica minutes bleeds time an hourglass

has thousands of forebears the henge pendulum clepsydra the earth's orbital hinge parts

a sundial down the center checks its six checks into bedlam at 6am a slow fog moving

has only stillness to envy to envoy my rockbottom bury-me-now foreversleeps fewer

the earth feels to us addicts always fewer rungs to climb down than from the heaven I needed

Winter Sketch

On the vanity, under the brass flea-market mirror,
beside incense & teapot, menagerie of the signified:
in blue pencil, robin's egg halves loud as cymbals.
Small brown glass vial of nitroglycerine I wafered
beneath your tongue to re-syncopate your pulse.
Bats' raw noses. Paint-flecked aprons of the elms.
Worry stones, river soft. The sun's smudged thumb
print (it reminds me of you) in a confabulist sky.
Seedpods, red-green & 3D, dehiscent, talismanic.
I have your blue-flame vase of tea roses framed here
in this room, still life on a stained tablecloth, heady
in their white defiance much longer than expected.
Yesterday, in a daydream-remembrance, a holdout:
breach torn in ether, red leaf letting go.

Wet Stars

you are slow rain fragrant in the eucalyptus

the night is slow rain, vindictive lightning

the street is wet blue & yellow-lamped

god is housing lights in clouds, housing predicaments

I can never see how I'll live ten more years

evening is a jade eucalyptus tree silent in no wind

the leaves fatigued under the streetlamps

children run out of cars straight indoors

I am going to the hammock to listen to Mazu

acceptance of the beginninglessness of things

sporadic ziggurats of lightning dissolve & erect

lean back into weightlessness, daylight's closed lids

remember me, what I said, what I wanted it to mean

The Poem You Asked For

The poem you asked for walks into therapy
by the hospital & remarks to the self, feeling
the cold tang of the sky seep into open, needy
places, what a fine day it is not to be writhing
in the ER waiting for more & more Xanax,
hallucinating axe murder, etc.—the poem you
asked for must deploy *etc.*, as in—has been to
detox, outpatient rehab, inpatient rehab, etc.—
has appeared in county jail, city jail, court-
ordered treatment, etc.—the poem you asked
for, you asked for it to probe *what are your
consequences*, line up your bona fides, but
the poem you asked for elides, now, & instead
shows you how, as a child, I spent recesses
slowly excavating gems in the playground dirt,
hunting arrowheads or geodes or any old stone
with a stripe of quartz, unearthing mycorrhizal,
chalk-white root systems under the influence
of fungi—or remember the network of black
widows behind the school's toolshed like beads
of ichor fallen & suspended amidst the dew?
The poem you asked for, finally, sidesteps,
backpedals, distracts, charms you & escapes—
you'll never hear from it again. Back down
in the valley living with the wild horses, lying
low, it's doing just fine.

Letter of Six Intentions

[Don't Recall]

you were standing in the corner of the room, white

you were across the firepit from me, mist

I don't know how to explain to you what I saw

many of you are expressed on other wavelengths now

a pond embraced the weight of the willow's hair

standing keen in the rain, a heron, watchful blade

[Don't Imagine]

eleven geese arrayed across the lacrosse field

each a datum, thought-forge, compass

sky the snarled undercarriage of the squall

the raingutter all summer askew, a clepsydra

white oleander dot parachuting through the porch

breathpink blossoms more open than ever before

[Don't Think]

your protection no longer so feverishly invoked

an arachnocracy forums above the ice-cream shop

matrilineal, they are taking their minutes in silk

has your soft hand rummaged much above the lintel?

like conflict & fear, you are always leaving & arriving

today under the wash of sun we are alive

[Don't Examine]

hearth-bellied intercessors, you who marrowed me

Mark, Margie, María, it was you with me in the night

& you, Aline, in white—& your tea roses

that your signal redshifts is of no concern

the moths, rubies, & seedpods offer augury

the best public broadcast is a coterie of birches

[Don't Control]

right effort has seen me set aside my will

my breath is my silk inheritance from you

sunlight calicoed the sweeping arms of oaks

& the squirrels received a bounty of Cheetos

years rent banjoing the derelict harp of my life

this is where I keep you, your hand atop my chest

[Rest]

I am accessing temples you may not know you have left

a jadethroat partook of the breath of my porch, a boon

yet truly tacking the canoe has yet to distill as instinct

the sunlight is a different god today

the hills & their blue prosperity

I have no future, I have this

PART III.

Antiquities

a beige layer
of meaning

settles over
our years

cruelty dims
earnest as

a baker
I tried

to sate you
yeast dust

flour chalk
the kiln

spat me out
pinker rawer

a miracle
a heresy

against time
which bends

around stars
like tongues

an archaeology
in cryo-sleep

my memories
swirl solar

around time
a satellite

flung from the oven
judicially

offering
daily I shed

my cellular memory
of you

I move through space
not entirely

willingly
tilting

my once lover
back gently

into the flame
of my eyes

Blue Loop

As we alcoholics know each escape is a return
a reversion a plea to renegotiate:

any capacity to do damage
entails intimacy with neglect.

There was a time when I did not feel this way—
when you held my hand & loved me—

much later I grew covetous & flew.

✦

There were omens: a raven's feather
with its blue sheen,

the hills & their blue prosperity—
I can never see how I'll live ten more years,

which is so selfish
it is perhaps more intolerable

than that I am I & you are you.
The trees restless, ripe.

Stop, & feel the planet in its death roll.
Lightning strikes & the ridges blaze.

Blue Loop

Evening is a jade eucalyptus tree silent in no wind,
            the sun an egg yolk on blue cloth.

            The star sings its night song, me:
when I fell out of time I fell out of this song.

In searching for the antecedent for myself
            I fear mistranslating myself:

I am nothing but everything I am not, see?
            Earth in its diadem, me on my path.

After I forget this, after my sister forgets this,
            after my mother & father forget this

will this still have happened to me?

White light enmeshes me each morning,
            each night pale light flattens me out.

In the kiln the vessel cracks & salt rushes in.

Blue Loop

It does not matter what we will be,
only what we refuse to be.

Here is my rain-white museum
where I was getting sober,

where I ransacked all practicing I've gleaned—
& yet there is always a flaw:

I am the bull in the meadow.
I am here, I remain.

Thirty-three months now on this walkabout
in the unattested silent, reverent place.

I move through space febrile & restless,
licking my soft parts, breaking & remaking new joints.

I am a needle shimmied into cork.
The sky darkens & I walk into dreams.

Blue Loop

The darkness floats, glacial, on larger bodies of dark:

> the part of the story where I emerge
> more benevolent & humble.

Lots of theories now I love:

> tomatoes like darkrooms
> detonate from inside out
>
> watch the sun's arms pump
> their nectar into flame.

Before I was together, I was prophecy:

> on the far horizon,
> smudge of superhot furnace
>
> & how long the body
> holds a fist within the gut.

Mark, Margie, María, it was you with me in the night:

> you are always leaving & arriving,
> like conflict & fear.

These poems are about you:

> the past you cannot see clearly,
> & the future you cannot see through.

In the valley living with the wild horses:

> this is where I keep you,
> your hand atop my chest.

Blue Loop

How to enter the mind: like a thief
entering an uninhabited house.

Glass flowers on a wet afternoon.

✦

All meaning is dissolving:
all singing is sorrow & remedy in time.

✦

I loved you there: being frantic,
being out of control,

a bone ball clacking
through night scenes.

✦

Lean back into weightlessness,
daylight's closed lids:

say to the frantic heart
you next.

An Effective Field Theory

I'm on the phone with my former companion
who has relapsed. Let's say *has been relapsing*
all year & is again starting over. I start over again
each morning, waking up from another dream

in which, like old friends, we go out on a date.
Near the end we kiss or embrace, then I meet
your new boyfriend, then I wake up. I wake
up & twenty geese fly overhead, unzipping

the sky & occupying the white-receiving field.
You wake up in darkness & go to the hospital.
Sutures, blood thinners, Xanax, who knows.
The field wakes up in a greyout with the sun

a white thumbprint, the creek a dead vein.
One tree in the foreground & behind—

✦

winter, & the stunned sky shellacs the breath of the living

porcelain sunlight glazes the battered torsos of the oaks

it does not matter what we will be, only what we refuse to be

everybody goes to rehab, some of us before we die

✦

                        I am in the wrong town pacing hours
in front of brownstones—

                        no doubt a prerequisite to learn god's name
to learn how in god's name we lived like that.

                              ✦

how to enter
the mind:

like a thief
entering
an uninhabited house

like one determined
to plunder
an ordinary stone

from an island
made entirely of gold

like a dream
for its own sake:

without desire
without judgment—
in need

                              ✦

Out of emptiness, out of need, breath is made.
Out of breath comes breath. Meditation:

to allow thought to parade, or to pose,
un-self-consciously, in front of the mirror of the mind.

To say to the frantic heart *you next*.

✦

Everybody Left the Party
If the Party Was Ever a Party
In This Ward
Medical Detox
But Had Given Up
My Grandmother Said
I'm Just Sad

But I Kept Singing, Unsure
Or the Silence beneath Phase
Every Inmate's Going Through
Got a Loss Kink
On Elegies
Oh Those Pills
Not Depressed

✦

Love is a sovereign. Time is very long.

✦

Thirty-three months now on this walkabout:
       earth in its diadem   me on my path

I am unsure for what cause I became intimately more afraid.

✦

You thought—you were sure—at some point you chose
       the subject matter of your life.

       My dear friend, a physicist, says the wonder
    of complexity is that it is uncomplicated.

    A man is an animal more intricate than dust,
       less intricate than whatever he thinks he is.

✦

I am afraid of going back. & yet more afraid,
having left you there, I will never see you again.

✦

We have more time than we expect
          & less than we need.

PART IV.

Authorities

geologic time
written off as a joke

on this continent yet
is how we got

among other crimes
sins unenumerable

this continent
I am hearing the arc of

the welder's torch
from the gutter

swollen with rainwash
yesterday it poured

all afternoon
mud bathtubs

neighborhood-wide
broaching the domiciles

the taking
like renewal

witnesses us
our brutality diaphanous

monoculturing the garden
tomatoes like darkrooms

rhizomes alight
angels aplenty

resounding & white
salamanders wobbling

their religion
rude to say cult

imbued in the groove of
stretchy eons

trickling down
to clog our coffers

the incitement
of jumping spiders

a matrilineal transparency
of faith

Meadow's Song

God, I've heard, has been looking for me.

Against memory's closed bedroom door—
       thermos & headlamp, the slow walk down

to the lime-slick cavernscape of *why I chose to do*
       those things I did.

✦

Pummeling through dreams of eternal inescape
       a malignancy, blown-out neon—

       inexplicable bruises. Nectar-gold
night-wound, Jupiter. Paper-white

       orchid's fanged womb.

✦

Last night an asteroid entered the atmosphere
       just overhead, blue-white, embraced by fire.

Like this stone I blink out & become a pebble
       in the meadow & you hold me

& imagine what I was in that place & time before—
       stubborn rock in a black sea of cold radio.

✦

Lying down to sleep an eight-hundredth
        inoculating sleep, a twenty-thousandth

        hour hung up in the wind to dry,
I remember you: I recall who rescued me.

✦

There's this creature here that isn't mine
        who cries out at night not to be returned.

Saturn Devouring His Son

Let us begin as a single grain,
        a mote alone in a galactic clamshell,
as the tongue of the universe licks
        fanatically at a bad tooth

      DIGITIZE—
        from *digit*
         from *digitalis*
          from *finger*
          from *discrete*

What we have to work with
        are some neutrinos,
some gravitons, some stretch marks
        in spacetime like the creases
leading to my armpits—

          from *dexterous*
         from *rectify*
         from *grab hold*
          from *render tactile*
           from *reduce to palm-sized*

      & yet there is always a flaw—
even the angels loved too much

          from *pummel*
         from *incise with pressure*
         from *x lbs. per square inch*
          from *arithmetic*
         from *prism*

      Because they taught us in physics class—
in classical mechanics—that power is just
        hard work over time

from *prison*
from *geometry of light*
from *geography of crease of skin*
from *skin*
from *the left hand alien to the right*

Not that the spirit oracles through the bone—

from *alien*
from *abacus*
from *binary*
from *twist of hair around index*
from *gently stroke loose from ego*

The darkness floats, glacial,
on larger bodies of dark—

from *conscious lacking directive*
from *tenderly*
from *tenderize*
from *break in*
from *bind*

My mouth: essays silence

from *cataract*
from *bowdlerize*
from *cauterize*
from *halt & catch fire*
from *eradicate cascade*

———————————

\>\>\>\>\>\>\>
& how

    long

       the body

          works

       to wax

    a splinter

\>\>\>\>\>\>\>\>\>\>\>\>\>
& how

    long

       the body

          kneads

       a fist

    within

the gut

\>\>\>\>\>\>\>\>\>\>\>\>\>\>\>\>\>\>
& how

    long

       the body

          holds

       its cup

    around

the shape

    you left

\>
& how

    long

       the body

          waits

       to be

    scraped

clean

Elsewhere's Rain

My father watches me drink from
the corner of the motel room—

his stubble his grey face
I don't know him

but for years he will
keep getting in—

he is grasping after
my hand hauling me

across the void
the earth drags through.

✦

Indigo hillside tidal wave,
wet stars luring tongues out of my interior—

the moon's white eye,
milk grin—

sky's cold atomic bonfire,
starlight more cleansing than rain.

✦

All that year I ran down to the river
hoping to sober

but waiting to die—
the river grew a mouth

& drank me, much later
I grew covetous & flew.

✦

There is a gleaming
& a concealing in this life,

an inner &
an outer proof.

✦

Great wheel of the world
with light-year spokes,

my planet an aquamarine
marble in a shooter's game.

✦

In the gutter, under
my toe, softer

than anticipated,
chickadee.

✦

Blue throat of daylight,
death's six-walled jade tomb.

✦

If life is not a miracle it is
a profound chemical emergence—

yet so often daybreak disappears
all I know of life on earth.

✦

Black door in the mountainside,
blue door in the blade forest—

white door interlocutor onto
red-door grey-flesh room.

✦

Stop, & feel the planet in its death roll—
which is meaner, gravity or light?

✦

When at last you departed from me
I became you, watched you bloom

in sadness toward me,
hid within pity's wide mouth

like a minor chord:
sovereign, defiant & true.

✦

From a secret place, suddenly,
clouds become what you want to see.

✦

My hands hymnal into cistern;
rainclouds blister into rain.

Unvisitable Stars

> *God break me out*
> *of this stiff life I've made.*
> —Jean Valentine, "Forces"

God dropped me, seed to divot, to
break back into bloomdom, sucked
me out of soul–Tupperware/petri dish,
out of immortality's white womb, said
of this protein suit make great ruckus on
this artless glassine grand plateau, caustic,
stiff I fell fast a searing white bead into
life already in my coveralls, so it's no wonder
I've fled the mending tasks—my annoyance
made the papers long before I got here.

Again for the sinners like me, for the callous, for God:
I know you, you spilled the cosmos over after a break
in the flask of the last cosmos—bet you're miffed at me,
this flagrant cadre of *me*, breeding suns like lilacs out
of star spit, more often glam out of haze, winter out of
turn, all the year winter, winter stars hibernating this
life away into shame—tell me stoic watcher why I stiff
up so many times a day, bristle, cower, flee—isn't life
for reticulation, budding—these mutant syntaxes I've
assembled, these impenetrable promises I've made.

The star is a talisman, I a diviner. The star is a golden flowering fruit & I its seed.
The star is a fixed warhead I wander around. The star sings its night song, me.
The star is the death of the star, I death of me. The star an atom cataract, I an atom.
The star is mournful light & I mournful thought. The star death-seen & I life-seen.
The star is a hole in the world & I a world in the whole—both seer & seen, I—me.

End of February, Helen Street

Dusk, & each cloud is one long sherbet javelin.
        Each house a boiled pastel, peeling
taupe. The neighbors are growing basement weed,
        or are night-shift nurses, or both.

Sundays, sundown is the only haven—for yet
        another week we are not dead.

The geese, returning, don't seem to like to cruise
        the metal sky but crave the crystal-wet grass.
The dogs all desperate & depressed.

How many people in this town—fifty thousand?—
        yet rarely in the park more than one or two
at a time. You want to get the hell out of here,
        but you want to stay.

Nightfall, & the moths draw down
        their inheritance of moonlight.

You are right not to want to be,
        not to want to be alone.

Life's Vibrancy Is Bright of Itself

[Moonlight in the dew]

this may be the last time that I write about you

there is room left here for one last new rule

yet this would not be my chosen art if I did not believe

      writing is preferable to not writing

in fact we are always losing

this demonstrates we are spending envy

then by our own volition or more likely by happenstance

      letting go

what is moonlight in the dew

I know dew before sunrise on my fingertip

dew in the moonlight is a release too soon

an overabundance of spending

      a hauntology outside-of-time

[Stars in a river]

I used to drive home late drunk

drive home drinking get home to finish the job

get home meant park by the Tennessee River

gravel roundabout

sometimes lovers were there in other cars

sometimes we were lovers there in my car

I stopped to watch the lights across the river

small & orange—six or ten—a jetty

they looked like far-off optimism

there was none on this side

the river was wide there

kayaking I crossed only once

[Snow on the pines]

this one I don't know well

no snow in Georgia

few pines left in Georgia

once we went to Gatlinburg Tennessee

I could hardly afford two nights

the water froze in the pipes & we switched rooms

I loved you there

we went up to the loft made for children

twin beds

made love there

snow in the darkness is a hauntology

[Clouds on a peak]

today you said you'd marry someone else

these poems are about you

I look up

clouds

no peak

the clouds sudsy pink & grey

some barely light pink—some vaguely grey

the sky behind is blue

this brightness reveals the wonder

it is 7pm on a Thursday

I cared for you for years

     & years after

I love you

     wish you peace

PART V.

Delinquencies

hard not to let you
ordain my guilt

open the ceiling to
see the blacklight ink

hard not to
want you to smother me

squeeze this life out
into the sky

I open
my mouth

my supplicant body
taffies into plasma

to prevaricate
a crab climbs out

pyroclast surges cools
my ice furnace

knuckled pink impasto
cyan ichor

rarefies into night wire
concertinas the heavens

petaling pleading
there is nothing

let me go let me go
to waste

in this world I want
more than nothing

each breath
less than the last

I have had & had
& been found ungrateful

my humanity retracted
planetless abandoned

any capacity
to do damage

by the cataract
to the core in my defense

entails intimacy
with neglect

to be cast out
is next to godliness

Epochs of the Son

the son at last collapsed into the father
the sun stumbled through wet black space

one single peal of fire molts singes emptiness
the great singular quilt bedspread of existence

the son roiling around on a Saturday morning
a pill bug an expanding nebula of material heat

on the far horizon smudge of superhot furnace
drifts across the cosmic all-duvet which bends

craters warps sunders time a gelatin billiards table
the son crashing off bumpers shellacked spheres

quaver a bone ball clacking through night scenes
remember the quark epoch I was dense plasma

a vast field spasming all excitement no interaction
seams swarming abuzz there was no binding me

to you so wrung I rang a piercing lacrimosa
pulled-apart stitches still reverberating to this day

less than a trillionth of a second yet unending
then in the next brief epoch before photons

atoms stability the in-between smithereens
of time witnessed near-total self-annihilation

Canopus in Blue Loop
Canopic urn, 1st century BCE

rain bruises the face of the river with envy, aluminum

rain a steaming shroud river a swift lead vest atop the watershed

mud—a clay urn weeping—folds into the wet clefts of the earth

pearling, petrochemicals plastic in the wet low folds of the earth

tracing your ridge of nose, contoured lip mound, mouth basin

no stance as maliced as the past, no supper room as polluted

✦

today I wished to look upon, caress, to hold your face

hear once more you sing your monosyncratic song

into the urn we folded your tissues, kidney, lung

folded into the clay urn your face, demeanor, breath

out of the unlipped clay urn emerge entropy, deified time

time a monostich of ducks, calm flotilla, panicked paddle foil

river of lead heavy water deuterium in its catacomb-green groan

we tremble atop the shifting liquid schist *like ducks in the time of ducks*

Kilning

April, dampen our mouths
 damage, whet my mind-axe

make me make something
 of roughness, grit

trauma slips, binds, we cannot
 shirk, avoid it

in the kiln the vessel cracks
 & salt rushes in

febrile & restless, licking
 our soft parts

breaking & remaking
 new joints

let me be taffy
 in your mouth

let me lie still
 shrinking

& around me you
 work, sing

Entropy

all meaning is dissolving

      clouds: then explain us

✦

water, which is flighty & unstable,
      clings to dust in an intermediary
      state, then dissolves, as you said

✦

bracketology, electromagnetic libation, night-
      sun, St. Elmo's fire, prairie man o' war

✦

a degree of belief should be rationally
      alterable given the availability of evidence

✦

even spacetime is emergent; we are early
      to the party of wave decay

✦

quanta: collapsed, we are dressing up as particles

✦

so then clouds are waves collapsing,
            water untethered from earth

✦

lecturer: is Nature singular or plural?

            that depends, where on my body
            are you placing your hands?

Ode

you: late flower

you: garnet-heart padma

you: say to me look, it will open into iris

me: scarlet-robed green shoot

you: lake island

you: sun-stroked afternoon

me: jeweled bee in your palm

you: high rolling plains summer thunder

me: each lightning strike of you crushes into gem

you: indefinite echo, voice-glove

me: sloshes back toward attainment

you: say to me no, don't

Cloud Resolves

Before I was, I was much less singular
Before I was together, I was prophecy

I am un-prophesying
I am re-solving to simplify

We do not know if change is an arrow
We do not know if change is absolute

Remember:

Each day you are assembling your life
Each day life is assembling you

When I fell out of time
I fell out of this song

Wherever you are, be well there

All singing is worship
All singing is sorrow & remedy in time

Cloud Absolves

The honeybees are ass-up in the bougainvillea,
                                        the robins frisky
& the ants are flinging open their cellar doors all over
                                        the neighborhood,
the sunlight a base layer of prime laid down.

I have the tendency to suggest we are defined
                                        by our ‹no›s,
that we become outlined entirely by our unique
                                        negative capability.
Perhaps—though the material my ‹no›s are cut & sewn from are
                                        violent yeses.

✦

Lots of theories now I love

                    The one where existence is

Transformative happenings

                    The one where it's threads

Yarns, webs—what are we

                    Wanting to feel connected to?

What are we hoping we are

                    Ever in the process of becoming?

✦

Two starlings hatching plans atop a metal fence
                                        in silk black
evening, streetlamp's corroding silver sodium near-silence
                                        between Jupiter
& moon. We will never see anything as it is,
                                        only late angles,
imperceptible how much had to combust to get to here.
                                        A night wind shakes
nothing through to nothing. I am glad not to know
                                        the twine between
me & everything—it may well be terrifying, unnatural,
                                        a god thing.

✦

You try to live between large & small,
                                        like a confession
written on a single page sealed in an envelope kept safe
                                        by a lover
on a shelf, brought down once or twice or never.

& yet to be extra-credible, thought of long after amidst
                                        strange, unmanageable
moments of impasse. To be the one who spoke daring,
                                        mystical truths.

✦

In searching for the antecedent for myself I fear mis-
                              translating myself.
I am nothing but everything I am not. See? Perhaps
                              you have witnessed
the uncanny quickness of the pounce & that the mouse does
                              not, unexpectedly,
play dead. I cannot think of anything more uncanny than
                              that I am I
& you are you. Yesterday around 8pm the sun an egg yolk
                              on blue cloth
& I simply could not believe *this is a star*.

✦

One yew tree in a field in the fog

                              Behind, one blue mountain
Behind that, one long, snaking river

                              Alongside it, grey loaf stones
Beside the tree in the field, a bull

                              I am the bull in the meadow
Bull in the field in the fog

                              Or am I the river?
I am here, I remain

                              Whether you approach or run
However you turn your head

✦

Do you know this one? Cloudy day,

                                    cloudy day,

cloudy day & then sun! Not the old silver sun,

                                    young blue sun,

greening the leaves & reddening the shutters,

                                    glory-hymn sun

the looker, lancer, topspin in the eyeball sun,

                                    Saturday morning

childhood Pine-Sol sun, diamantine tarmac sun,

                                    bedroom window

crystal, shine & retribution, skull-&-moon sun,

                                    afterimage smoke-

white, blood-wet earth sun, sun-warm pour into

                                    your open hand

grasping me death-tight, nowhere left to hide, no night

                                    into which to steal.

✦

Don't you like the way small drops of rain seem not to fall (screaming, down) through the sky at all, but simply to be expanding, elastic circles in puddles on the street? This is not unlike the way we see light & particles as it relates to their greater being: we see waves strike & broaden, while the stuff itself is rain-strings tied to cloudheads tied to aquifers of bits. I am so glad there is so much I do not know. Life is hard, sad, & futile—but we live it in this impossibly complex, unlikely singing place. So exquisite how, at some point, life began & nothing in existence bowed down. The many-colored iridescent radioactive hearths went on blazing in defiance of nothing, a billion billion particles raging beyond our scope to comprehend.

White light enmeshes me each morning, each night pale light flattens me out. Wish we had not been abandoned into this life.

I Was Here Before & Will Be Here Again

I watch a time-lapse animation of the Appalachians
squigging up into existence over tens or hundreds
of millions of years. How colossal were the sloths
&, consequently, how slow? They appeal to me.
Lightning strikes & the ridges blaze & perhaps
the sloths escape or not. There are pain-deep blue
lakes & scaled fish in them & this is the earth.
Myopic, we concocted heaven, too naïve to see
that we are born into it, we are the angels, tested
under the same rubric of all tests: pretend this is
real. Don't you rub up against the set variables,
sliding scales, are you not sure in quiet moments
that, even if you don't know which it is, your life
is a language or ethics problem leading to a single
answer alone? You know your answer already yet
feel compelled to evince a choice because as we
choose, again & again, we are learning which
conditions correlate with whom choosing what.
This is called literature, & the exam confirms
the hypothesis: I am everyone & I choose me.
There was a time when I did not feel this way,
when you held my hand & loved me, then it
felt like I could die, evaporate calmly into mist.
Sometimes now the sky darkens & I walk into
the dreams where I see you thinking *lead us not;
deliver us.* Wish that I could keep just the won
wisdom of arrival & not recall the journey here.
Do you remember the great flames? They will
return, you will see that they were always around,
in the adjacent room that's forever been there but
that you'd never dreamed of opening. Open it:
the lover sits at a small table sipping tea, doesn't
speak as you walk past them to the window above
the sink, unsash it to harsh light. When you turn
around they are not there. But they are not gone.

Notes

First epigraph from "Art and Life," from *Time and Materials* by Robert Hass. Copyright © 2007 by Robert Hass. Used by permission of HarperCollins Publishers.

The epigraph attributed to the Buddhist monk Tilopa was translated by Lex Hixon in *Mother of the Buddhas*, published by Quest Books.

Definition of a blue loop is adapted from the Wikipedia entry on the subject.

"Juniper" refers to the Ware Collection of Blaschka Glass Models of Plants, located at the Harvard Museum of Natural History.

"Hostilities," "Antiquities," "Authorities," & "Delinquencies" are cleave poems: to be read either across or down.

"Only the Earth" is a double golden shovel.

"Wet Stars" quotes the poem "Cedar Fires" by Arthur Sze & the teachings of Mazu, from *Classics of Buddhism and Zen, Volume One: The Collected Translations of Thomas Cleary*, published by Shambhala.

"The Poem You Asked For" shares a title with a poem by Larry Levis.

"Letter of Six Intentions" hangs upon the Six Nails of Tilopa, as translated by Ken McLeod.

Each "Blue Loop" is a self-cento composed of lines from this book.

"An Effective Field Theory" borrows from Mipham Rinpoche in "The Essence of Wakefulness" as translated by Erik Pema Kunsang: "Be free from hope or fear about whether or not thoughts do occur—just like a thief entering an uninhabited house. . . . Just as you cannot find any ordinary stones on an island of gold."

"*Saturn Devouring His Son*" begins in the cadence of the poem "Five Psalms" by Mark Jarman & later echoes "Spring Drawing 2" by Robert Hass. Power = work divided by time.

"Unvisitable Stars" is a phrase in the sequence "The Messenger" by Jean Valentine. The first two parts of my poem are a golden shovel using a phrase from Valentine's poem "Forces."

"Life's Vibrancy Is Bright of Itself": This phrase appears in a poem on Silent Illumination by Hongzhi. The subtitles & the phrase "this brightness reveals the wonder" also appear in the text as translated by Hakuun Barnhard of Wolk en Water (Cloud and Water) hermitage.

"Canopus in Blue Loop" quotes "The Asians Dying," a pacifist protest poem by W. S. Merwin.

"Kilning" quotes "Stray Paragraphs in April, Year of the Rat" by Charles Wright.

Acknowledgments

Grateful acknowledgment is made to the following journals and outlets in which some of these poems first appeared, often in different forms: *The Account, Best New Poets, Fugue, Green Verse: An Anthology of Poems for Our Planet, Overheard, poets.org, Taco Bell Quarterly, & West Trade Review*.

Immense gratitude to those from whom my writing has received material support: The Carole M. Weinstein Scholarship Fund & the Friends of *Blackbird* Fund at Virginia Commonwealth University, The Lieberman Fund at Binghamton University, & the Morehead-Cain Foundation at the University of North Carolina at Chapel Hill.

Thanks first to all the students I have ever had the unquantifiable benefit to have taught. All teachers know we learn the most from our students.

To those who have shared the writerly journey with me any portion of the way—Michael Robinson, Katherine Mooney Brooks, Sarah Nelson Rupp, Ciera Higginbotham, Brandie Gray, Caitlin Wilson, Jordan Franklin, Alycia Calvert, Ella Flores, Liz Young, & everyone else—I am so thankful for you.

To my teachers—Beth Wilson, Daniel Wallace, Randall Kenan, Gabrielle Calvocoressi, Gregory Donovan, David Wojahn, & Kathy Graber—I would not be the writer or the person I am without any one of you.

To those who worked with me, often laboriously, on these poems—Colin Bailes, Suzanne Richardson, Shannon Hearn, Derek Ellis, Tina Chang, & Joe Weil—I cannot thank you enough for helping me see what I strain to see & say what I mean to say.

I will all my life be grateful to Chelsea Dingman for offering this book, then only a manuscript, time, energy, & grace.

To those I love who have gone on ahead—Grandma Georgia, Grandma & Pop, Mark, Margie, Wendy—these poems are always for you.

Lastly, to my mother, father, and sister: I love you. Thank you for being my lights in the world.